Writing An Irresistible Ebook In One Weekend:
The New Method To Write A Book Readers Adore, Ready To Sell Monday Morning.

TABLE OF CONTENTS

INTRODUCTION. 4

Quality Is The #1 Priority. 5

Here Is The Program. 6

A Reusable Process. 8

MODULE #1: FIND A TOPIC THAT WILL SELL. 9

Choosing The Right Type Of Book. 9

Your Ebook Must Bring A Solution To A Problem. 10

The More Important The Problem You Are Going To Solve Is, The More Profitable Your Ebook Will Be. 11

Analyze The Statistics Of Your Niche Market. 13

One Word About The Length Of Your Ebook. 15

MODULE #2: CREATE THE STRUCTURE OF YOUR EBOOK. 16

List Five Major Obstacles That Prevent Your Customers From Solving Their Problem. 17

List The Possible Solutions You Are Going To Give To Your Customers. 19

Build The Plan Of Your Ebook. 22

Rephrase The Titles And Techniques Of Your Modules. 25

Create The Structure Of Your Ebook. 30

MODULE #3: START WRITING YOUR EBOOK. 32

Basic Rules To Write Efficiently. 33

Write Two To Three Times Faster With Heminghway's Technique. 34

Insert Comments If Needed. 36

MODULE #4: EDIT YOUR EBOOK. 37

Basic Rules To Edit Efficiently. 38

Use Examples. 40

Have Your Ebook Reviewed By Choosing Well Your Reviewers. 41

MODULE #5: FINALIZE YOUR EBOOK. 44

Create A Professional Cover Without Technical Skills Within Ten Minutes. 45

Convert Your Ebook Into The Right Format.......................51

CONCLUSION. 53

BONUS: WHERE AND HOW TO SELL YOUR EBOOKS....54

Create Your Sales Page. 54

Use Online Self-Publishing Platforms. 55

ABOUT THE AUTHOR. 56

CREATIONS FROM THE SAME AUTHOR. 57

INTRODUCTION.

Congratulations, you are now part of a minority of people who are really going to know how it is possible to write an irresistible ebook that readers will adore in just one weekend, and that is ready for sale on Monday morning.

You are holding in your hands a realistic method that you simply need to apply step-by-step to create your ebook from A to Z, in an accelerated manner.

Quality Is The #1 Priority.

But don't fool yourself. If timeliness is important, the quality of your ebook is even more important.

And that's what makes all the difference between this method and others that promise you to write an ebook in an hour or less.

This kind of achievement can however be possible, if you are doing patchwork and you just copy and paste articles that you find here and there, to ultimately create something that looks like anything but a book that people will adore.

The goal of this method is certainly not to show you how to do this kind of tasteless, low quality ebook and without any interest or respect for readers.

This method will allow you to make original content. The kind of content that makes an ebook irresistible and becomes best-seller in your market.

Everything will be done not in an hour or less like dreamsellers happily promise you, but in one weekend. To have your ebook ready for sale on Monday morning.

Here Is The Program.

This book is composed of five modules that you can simply follow step-by-step. Here are all the amazing things you are going to discover:

Module # 1
By the end of the first module, you will have already found a topic or concept that will work for your ebook.

You will also have the answer to several key questions that you might have, such as the right length an ebook should be, or why you do not need to be an expert on the subject you are going to write about or a professional writer.

Module # 2
At the end of the second module, you will have created the whole structure of your ebook and you will have dispatched it in your working document.

Module # 3
No later than the end of module #3, your ebook will be fully written, in draft mode.

You will master in particular Hemingway's writing technique, which will allow you to write two to three times faster than now with less efforts and with a style that will make your readers vibrate with emotion.

Module # 4

At the end of module #4, your book will be completely edited and your content frozen. It will only remain to create a cover and turn the book into the right format.

Module # 5

At the end of the fifth module, your ebook will be finalized and ready for sale.

You will see in particular how you can professionally create the cover of your ebook in just ten minutes, without any technical skill and without spending a single dollar.

You will also discover how you can easily convert it into the right digital format, to make it ready for sale.

Bonus.

At the end of this book, I offer you a bonus section that will give you the tools and the most profitable and effective ways to sell your ebook on the Internet simply and immediately.

A Reusable Process.

If you correctly apply each step of this method, you will in the end have created an irresistible ebook in an accelerated manner, and ready to sell.

Unlike other digital books, your content will be original and of quality, and your readers will adore it.

The big advantage is that you could reuse the same process you are about to learn here to write as many ebooks as you want, whenever you have a free weekend to do it.

This way, you could progressively build a stream of passive income that will grow with each new book you create, at your own pace.

Let's start right now with the first module.

MODULE #1: FIND A TOPIC THAT WILL SELL.

Choosing The Right Type Of Book.

In the world of ebooks, there are two main categories: fiction books and non-fiction books.

Fiction books are generally novels or short stories. Fiction books are the most random in terms of success, because it is very difficult to know in advance whether or not the book will sell.

Then, there are the non-fiction books, which deliver information in an infinity of topics. You have travel books, cooking books, well-being books, educational books, books about psychology or medicine, art and culture, science and technology, etc.

Among the non-fiction books, there is the "solution ebooks" category.

These ebooks are created to provide a solution to a problem people face on a particular topic among the infinity of topics that exist.

These are practical books that explain how to do this or that, how to solve this or that problem.

This is the type of ebooks we will choose, because it is much easier to know if it will sell or not (of course, on condition that you have the good method).

Your Ebook Must Bring A Solution To A Problem.

As we have just seen, the easiest ebooks to sell are the "solution ebooks", in other words those who bring a concrete solution to a defined problem.

What you need to know is that you will not present your ebook as an ebook, but as a solution to a problem.

You are going to focus on your book content, not on the container.

This way, you will be able to sell more and at a higher price: your customers will not buy a PDF ebook, they will buy the solution to their problem.

Thus, they will be more inclined to spend more money.

A client who goes to a DIY store is not seeking a drill, he is looking for a way to make a hole.

Your customers are not looking for a book, but for a solution to their problems.

The real value of the container (ebook) has nothing to do with the value perceived by the customer, who is 100% focused on the content.

The More Important The Problem You Are Going To Solve Is, The More Profitable Your Ebook Will Be.

We can classify problems into two main categories:

The Major Problems.

Examples of ebooks that solve a major problem:

A method to lose weight, to save your marriage, to get out of debt...

These books are changing the lives of your customers. They get them out of a big mess, they suppress a big problem that makes their lives a misery, and that's why they are by far the most profitable.

However, you will have to face tough competition in such types of markets.

The Secondary Problems.

These are less important problems to solve and are related to a secondary desire.

For example: learning to swim, playing the piano, using a design software, etc.

These books are less profitable than those who solve a major problem, but you can much more easily outrun your competitors if your marketing is well made.

The creation of such an ebook will also be much easier for you. Simply take a theme that you like or that you know (playing the piano, using a photo editing software, maintaining a vegetable garden, etc.), and you will not necessarily need to document yourself a lot to create a quality product.

A simple way to find ideas is to list your own problems and desires, including those you've managed to solve or to eliminate.

Beware Of The Trends.

Furthermore, I strongly recommend you to find a problem that is not related to a temporary trend but always remain true in the long run.

This will ensure you that your ebook will always sell as well as now in five or ten years because the need will always exist.

Indeed, you're more likely to sell for a long time a method to learn how to scuba dive rather than a method to understand the latest features of the iPhone 6.

The first method does will never go out of fashion and you will still make as many sales as now in thirty years, while the second will be obsolete after six months when a new phone will come out, and then you will be selling almost nothing.

Analyze The Statistics Of Your Niche Market.

Before you decide to choose a subject or another for your ebook, it is essential to gather numerical data to assess your chances of success.

Write down a minimum of twenty topics ideas, and analyze their statistics. You could then select the best one.

The goal is to identify markets where users are making enough searches to guarantee you will have enough potential customers, while avoiding areas where the competition is too tough.

Use Google Keyword Planner.

Google Keyword Planner (https://adwords.google.com/KeywordPlanner) is the reference and must-use tool to analyze how interesting is a particular niche market.

It allows you to know the number of times a word or phrase is searched in Google search engine every month.

The best is of course to find keywords that people search a lot, but on which there is little or no competition.

As you can imagine, these golden nuggets are hard to find.

You can just choose words that have an important number of searches and where competition is average.

Compare the keywords related to the topic ideas you listed for your ebook, in order to choose those who seem the most interesting according to the data found on Google Keyword Planner.

Use Google Trends As A Supplement.

A good additional way to test your ideas is to use the Google Trends Service (http://www.google.com/trends/), which gives you historical statistics of the number of searches for a given keyword.

This is very useful in order to know if a topic is linked to temporary trend, if its becoming more and more popular or, on the contrary, if the topic starts to become obsolete.

One Word About The Length Of Your Ebook.

Now that you have selected the topic of your ebook and before moving to the next module, you may wonder what is a good length for your ebook.

The answer is that the length of your ebook does not really make sense because this kind of question still associates the value of your book to its container, to quantity.

You should know that the value of your ebook has nothing to do with the expertise you have, the time you spend writing it, or its length.

The value of your ebook has only to do with the value perceived by the customer who will judge it on its ability to solve his problem effectively, and not on its length.

Moreover, many people will prefer a short book of about forty or fifty pages which provides a clear and practical solution, rather than a book of two hundred pages full of useless theory leaving them with their problem still unsolved.

Always keep in mind that most people who are looking for solving a problem are in a hurry and want to solve it as quickly as possible.

If your book is too long, they will likely move on to something else or worse, they may perceive you as unable to explain things in a clear and concise manner.

MODULE #2: CREATE THE STRUCTURE OF YOUR EBOOK.

Now that you have chosen the topic of your ebook thanks to the previous module, you will have created by the end of this module the complete structure of your ebook with a detailed plan, composed of irresistible titles and subtitles.

Before you start writing, you must indeed first have created your working document, and have a clear plan of what you are going to write. Otherwise, you might quickly get lost and come up with a mediocre result and in a lot more time.

In addition, it is necessary to make your titles and subtitles impactful so that they grab readers' interest. For example, if the title of your book is not attractive, all the content of your book will be useless because nobody will take the time to read it.

However, if the title of your ebook is irresistible and if each theme and sub-theme of your ebook is formulated in a way that adds even more excitement and interest, it is likely that people will not resist for long before buying it.

Just follow these steps in order to create the structure of your ebook.

List Five Major Obstacles That Prevent Your Customers From Solving Their Problem.

You are going to list five most annoying and major obstacles that make it difficult for your customers to solve their problem and get what they want (of course related to the topic of your ebook, chosen in module # 1).

The obstacles are often the same: time, money, education, physical or psychological effort.

Let's take some examples.

Example 1:
Suppose the ebook subject you have chosen in module # 1 is to learn to master Photoshop.

One obstacle that prevents your customers from mastering Photoshop is that as soon as you open Photoshop, there are so many tools available that it is very difficult to know which one to use.

Another obstacle is that your customers may not have the time to learn all of the thousands of tools available in Photoshop before managing to draw a basic shape or to blur on a picture.

Example 2:
Suppose the ebook subject you have chosen in module # 1 is about how to seduce a woman in order to stop being single.

One of the main obstacles your customers face to achieve this goal is certainly shyness, lack of confidence.

Another obstacle may be that they don't have enough money to pay a dating agency or to subscribe to a dating website.

Before you move on to the next section, list five major obstacles that prevent the most your customers from solving the problem that your ebook will solve.

List The Possible Solutions You Are Going To Give To Your Customers.

Now that you have identified five major obstacles your customers face, you are going to make a list of the possible solutions you are going to give them, and that solve the five major obstacles you have just listed.

In other words, you are going to list the possible solutions that will require a minimum amount of time, a minimum of money, a minimum of education, a minimum of efforts, in order to overcome the five obstacles you have listed.

You will list these options using these three steps:

1- List The Things You Already Know.

Take a sheet and make a list of a maximum of ideas, tools, technologies, techniques, exercises you can give people, who will help them solve their problem without going through the five major difficulties and obstacles listed previously.

List all these little things, these funny and smart tricks that you already know, that you have read, heard or seen on TV, that shine, intrigue and arouse curiosity.

The idea is to make a list with a maximum of these tricks.

2- Make A Brainstorm To Find Some Creative Shortcuts.

Now that you have listed all the stuff you had "in stock" in your memory, you may still need more tips to give people in order to provide them the solution they need.

So you're going to make a brainstorm to find creative shortcuts, new tricks you have not listed and that will provide a complete solution to their problem.

Once you are running out of ideas, you can help yourself using external resources.

3- Use External Resources.

A great way is to go for example on various forums related to the topic of your ebook and see the conversations between users, the questions and answers.

One of the main general forums is Yahoo Answers (https://answers.yahoo.com/). Its main advantage is that its high volume of daily visits provides a relevant overall picture of the most frequently asked questions.

Another good way is to search for popular blogs related to your theme and view the tips and tricks that circulate in the articles.

If you plan to write more books later, a good idea is to sign up to their different newsletters. This way, you will certainly see things that are not necessarily visible to the general public, and that will serve you for your next ebook.

Another way a bit 'under the counter', is to go to Amazon and look at the table of contents of best selling competing books, using the "look inside" feature. It can give you ideas to help you complete your list of tricks.

You should know that Amazon is by far one of the most visited sites. This is enough to say that if a book is in the best sellers, that means it surely contains some very interesting things you could certainly use to get inspiration.

There are many other external resources, such as magazines in bookstores or electronic magazines.

Build The Plan Of Your Ebook.

Once you have created a long list of possible solutions that gathers all the tips, techniques and tricks that you will give to your customers to solve their problem, it's time to organize this list in the form of a plan.

I advise you to organize your plan in a maximum of seven parts. Beyond that, it becomes more difficult for people to follow the steps and they usually lose the overall vision of the set up of the solution.

A good average consists in making an introduction followed by four or five parts.

If possible, avoid calling "chapters" the different parts of your ebook, which often sounds low-cost and cheap for a solution ebook.

Prefer terms such as modules, steps or days if you offer a program in days.

Create a plan that you will organize in chronological order, taking people by the hand from A to Z, from the situation they are now up to the full resolution of their problem.

Create each module around a sub-theme or sub-part that can also be a day or a big step:

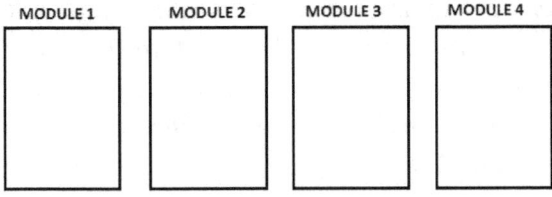

For each module, you are going to list all the techniques and tricks that you will provide your readers, drawing them from the list of possible solutions you have just created.

Note: you may find that you don't necessarily need all the techniques and tricks you have listed. In this case, you could use the remaining techniques for your future ebooks.

And second thing, you are going to specify the physical, concrete and if possibly numerical result that the reader should get at the end of each module:

MODULE 1

- Technique X
- Trick Y
- Tip Z
- etc...

- Concrete result at the end of the module

So when you will present your plan in your sales pitch you could say:

"At the end of the first module, you will already get this result. It remains to be seen this and that thing. And in the second module I'll teach you this and this technique, and at the end of the second module, you will already have this particular thing in place in your life, that specific result, etc."

Then, you will simply need to present the plan of your ebook to really make people want to buy.

Rephrase The Titles And Techniques Of Your Modules.

Now that your plan is done, it is time to rephrase the titles and techniques of the different modules of your plan, as well as the general title of your book.

The reason is purely for a marketing purpose, because the main title of your book and the titles and names of the techniques of your modules should be attractive and impactful enough to capture the attention and interest of your customers.

Remember that a main title that does not grab the customer's attention is a book that will not be purchased, and thus not read.

That's why the stake of the main title is huge, and you can miss many sales if you do not give it the attention it deserves.

Do this exercise to test your main title:

Put yourself in place of a potential customer and ask yourself if you would want to open your ebook and discover what's inside just by reading the title.

If the answer is no, it means that you have to find a stronger headline that will really capture your attention.

Two proven techniques to obtain an irresistible main title:

One of the best copywriters Gary Bencivenga gives this formidable formula to create a title that captures attention and generates the interest of the reader:

Benefit + Curiosity = Interest

If your headline promises at least one benefit and creates curiosity, then it will generate the reader's interest and you will have won the game.

As the formula shows, the greater the benefit and the element of curiosity are, the higher the reader's interest will be.

There are countless ways to get a winning title.

In general, a title that promise specific and numerical results is highly appreciated.

For example: "How to go from twenty to zero cigarettes in seven days" or "the secret method to remember a complicated poem in 2 minutes."

Another way to find a compelling title is to use this formula:

Result X, without Y

"**Result**" is what people want the most in your niche. For example, "master Photoshop like a pro."

"**X**" is the obstacle, the main difficulty your readers must deal with.

"**Y**" is a structure with a frame : in general a timeframe or a frame using various numbers (money, weight, distance, temperature, etc).

Some examples:

- Become a piano expert without knowing anything about solfeggio, in three weeks.

- How to speak French fluently being bad at languages, in seven days.

- Create your professional video without any equipment, with one dollar.

Do the same with the titles of your modules.

In addition to the main title of your ebook, also rephrase the titles of your modules to make them attractive and grab attention. Just trust your imagination, and if you lack ideas, you can also use the principles above to create them.

How to rephrase the techniques mentioned in your modules.

Finally, rephrase the name of the techniques listed in each of your modules.

The idea is to give them a name that does not exist anywhere else to make every technique, every tip, every trick you've listed appear as something you personally own.

You just have to invent a name, it could be something very simple.

Some examples:

- If you talk about a promotional technique consisting in gradually increasing the price of a product, you can rename it "the multiple stairs promotional technique"

- If you talk about a trick allowing people to instantly divide by two the number of cigarettes smoked without being in withdrawal, you can rename it "the tip of the cut packet".

- If you talk about a way to kiss a girl within the first thirty minutes of a date without getting shot down, you can rename "The Dom Juan's flash kissing method".

If you do that, you'll find it extremely easy to sell your ebook when you will then be promoting it.

Imagine having twenty techniques rephrased with proprietary names like the ones above.

There is nothing more attractive and more effective to stimulate the curiosity of your readers when you will list all these techniques in your sales letter. You could say for example:

- The multiple stairs promotional technique that will allow you to multiply by three your sales without paying more publicity.

- The tip of the cut packet that makes you instantly divide by two the number of cigarettes you smoke without ever being in withdrawal.

- The Dom Juan's flash kissing method that will give you the power to successfully kiss a girl within the first thirty minutes of your date without getting shot down.

Now take all the techniques listed in each module, and rephrase them with a name that does not exist anywhere else, and that will make you be the owner of these techniques.

Create The Structure Of Your Ebook.

Once your plan is finished and once you have rephrased the main title of your ebook, the titles of your modules and techniques listed in each module, you are now going to create the structure of your ebook.

Create a document in your word processor and write the titles and the names of the techniques of your different modules (that can be considered as subtitles), each one at the top of a blank page.

For example, if your first module is composed of eight techniques, you are going to write the title of module # 1 at the top of a blank page, and the title of the first technique of that module at the top of another blank page, and the title of the second technique of the same module at the top of a new blank page, etc.

So, you have now created the structure of your ebook, which is composed of a detailed plan with titles and names of techniques that are extremely attractive.

If you are afraid of not remembering the content you will need to write inside each module or inside each technique, you can also list your ideas or talking points on each one of these blank pages, without making sentences.

These points will serve you as a guide when you will start writing your ebook, to know exactly what to write in each part. But these points are optional if you are already familiar with your subject and know exactly what to write for each module and each technique.

It is now time to start writing your ebook; this is what we are going to see in the next module.

MODULE #3: START WRITING YOUR EBOOK.

At the end of this module, you will have written your whole ebook, in draft mode.

You will not have to worry anymore about how to write or how to formulate your sentences. Your writing style will be captivating, and you will write faster than 90% of people and with less efforts.

For that, you are going to discover the basic rules to write effectively, and also the technique of Ernest Hemingway that will allow you to divide by two or three of your writing time, increase the quality of your writing and diminish the efforts provided by your brain.

Basic Rules To Write Efficiently.

Take your book from the beginning and write for each module a first version by developing the key points and ideas that are listed.

Write quickly, just as if you were talking to someone in front of you.

The best is to imagine yourself talking to a friend.

It'll decomplex you, and you will see that your style will be much more natural.

And it's by being natural that you will manage to express emotion, passion, and that you will make all things exciting. Not by being reserved or by censoring yourself, as we often do in front of strangers.

Use short sentences and simple words and go to the essentials.

Remember that you are not here to write a novel but to offer a concrete solution to your customers' problem.

So do not look to make beautiful figures of speech, nor to look like an extremeley smart person by using complex and intelletual words. This is not what your customers expect from you.

It may even make things more difficult and boring to read, or even make you appear as someone who is not able to teach others in a simple way.

Write Two To Three Times Faster With Heminghway's Technique.

Once you start writing a module, don't stop at the end of each sentence to reread or analyze it.

Follow word for word this technique of the writer Ernest Hemingway that holds in one sentence:

"Write Drunk, Edit Sober"

Let's be clear: this does not mean you must start drinking whiskey or rum before starting to write. Absolutely not.

It means that once you start writing, you must absolutely avoid stopping along the way to analyze and correct each one of your sentences. Never.

In this way, you will unleash your inspiration and spontaneity allowing the right hemisphere (creative) of your brain to express itself without interruption.

Perhaps you already know that the brain has two hemispheres: the right hemisphere handles creativity, the left hemisphere handles rational analysis.

If you stop at the end of a sentence to proofread and correct it, it is as if you stopped the momentum of your creative right brain to activate your analytical left hemisphere.

Then as soon as you move to the next sentence, you must again stop your analytical left hemisphere to restart your creative right hemisphere.

It is as if you had to paint in blue two small bedrooms, and you stopped your paint roller every ten inches to go to the other room.

You lose time and it's very tiring.

You would go much faster to first paint the first room in blue entirely, then to start the second, rather than permanently going from one room to the other.

Your brain works the same way. By stopping at every sentence to reread and correct it, you lose a lot of time and you get tired unnecessarily.

So write without stopping, and do not worry about mistakes or badly formulated phrases that you leave behind, you will have all the time you want to correct and edit them later (it will be seen in the next module).

For now, the only goal is to turn your lists of points and ideas into text paragraphs in draft mode without worrying about editing.

Insert Comments If Needed.

This should not normally happen, but if you notice while writing that you still need to add information you do not have on hand, simply insert a comment in color and italics in order to easily come back later, then continue to write without stopping.

Once all your book is written and you have added all the information you wanted in the parts where you left comments, you have your entire ebook ready in draft mode.

The next module will show you how to properly edit your ebook.

MODULE #4: EDIT YOUR EBOOK.

At the end of this module, your ebook currently in draft mode will be fully edited.

You will now be able to use the analytical left hemisphere of your brain, which will be perfect for this editing step.

You will discover the basic rules to edit efficiently. People often think that editing only means correcting the spelling mistakes, but it's much more than that.

Editing also takes into account the length of the lines or the maximum size a paragraph should be to make the reading easier. You will see all the rules to know about this subject.

You will also see how to easily make your ideas understood and etch them permanently in people's memory. Moreover, it is often because of that that people will remember your ideas.

You'll also see how to select your audience correctly in the rereading step, which is optional but gives you the opportunity to add important things you would have forgotten or rephrase some parts, before making your ebook available to the general public. Indeed, what seems clear and comprehensive to us is not necessarily the case for others.

By applying these principles, your ebook will then be of an exceptional quality that will shine through on every page.

Basic Rules To Edit Efficiently.

Take your book from the beginning and reread it module by module.

For each module, correct all your spelling, grammatical and conjugation mistakes.

Rephrase badly formulated sentences.

Replace the words that are too often used by synonyms to avoid redundancy and to give more colors to your sentences.

Make sure paragraphs are linked logically and in a natural way. When you read, you should never wonder why a paragraph is here. Everything should flow naturally so that your readers never lose the thread of your ideas.

Try as much as possible to write one idea per sentence. If a sentence has two ideas, then cut it into two shorter sentences.

Do not forget also to aerate your text by skipping lines between paragraphs to make the reading more comfortable.

Some researchers such as François Richaudeau, Miles A. Tinker or Donald G. Patterson have aslo studied the good length text lines and pragraphs should have to maximize the understanding and the reading speed.

Studies show long paragraphs should be avoided. If we take the example of a sales letter, paragraphs of more than six lines - or more than 80 words - are considered too long.

For the length of text lines, a good average is between 50 and 80 characters, including spaces.

Use Examples.

Use this editing step to also enrich your ebook with concrete examples to illustrate your ideas.

Use examples that come from your personal experience, from the experience of famous people, quote a passage from a book or a film that marked you.

In short, tell stories and give concrete examples, because it is often the anecdotes that remain etched in the memory of the reader and allow him to easily understand an idea.

Once you went through all your ebook and applied all the editing rules you have just seen, reread it as many times as necessary and refine your ebook a bit little more each time until you are convinced you have optimized your text to the maximum.

Have Your Ebook Reviewed By Choosing Well Your Reviewers.

This step is optional, because for your book to be ready for sale in one weekend, it is unlikely that all your reviewers will be available at the same moment to review it immediately.

That being said, if you can wait a little bit longer than a weekend, having your book reviewed by some other people will certainly be of great help.

Indeed when you have your head to the grindstone, you do not necessarily see some errors and imperfections that will seem obvious to people who discover your book for the first time.

So, it's better to have your book reviewed now rather than starting to see negative feedbacks and comments by the general public on the mistakes they see.

You can also decide to publish it immediately without making this extra step, and then to update it in a second edition, once all the reviewers will have given you their feedback and once you will have made all the necessary modifications to your book.

To make this review, choose people who belong to the audience targeted by your ebook, mentioning them that their opinion is important to you because they represent the typical profile of your future readers.

If your book is targeting computer experts, you are not going to ask someone who barely knows to use a computer to review your book.

Similarly, if your book is targeting men only, you are not going to ask women to review it.

Or if it targets a young audience, you're not going to find reviewers among the grandfathers and grandmothers in a retirement home.

On the contrary, if your book is intended for beginners in a particular field, look for people who have little or no knowledge in that field.

For example, if your book is a method to quickly learn how to play the guitar, ask people who do not know how to play to review your book.

Ask each of your readers what they did not understand, what could be improved, if other missing topics should be addressed or if some points deserve to be explained differently, and make corrections if necessary.

At this stage, your ebook is now normally completely edited.

These editing rules are important to apply. Otherwise, you might not maximize the quality and the perceived value of your book, even if your content is excellent.

In the last module, you are going to see how to finalize your ebook to make it ready for sale.

You will see how to create in minutes a cover that will make your customers green of envy without any technical skills in design, and you will see the different formats you can use to convert your ebook.

MODULE #5: FINALIZE YOUR EBOOK.

Congratulations, you've come a long way and you have already well advanced.

It only remains to finalize your ebook and at the end of this module, your ebook will be ready for sale.

You will have created in minutes a cover for your ebook that will look great even if you have no technical skills.

For most people, creating a book cover is an incredible hassle, especially when one does not know how to do it. Many spend entire days or are outsourcing for hundreds of dollars, or take months learning how to use a complex software like Photoshop.

You are going to discover in the next pages how to avoid all these problems and within ten minutes, you will have your beautiful and professional looking cover made, and without spending a single dollar.

You will also have converted your ebook into the appropriate digital format with simple tools, and it will be ready to sell.

Create A Professional Cover Without Technical Skills Within Ten Minutes.

Creating an ebook cover is often a big pain for most people who do not know how to do it.

Many people do not know how to use a drawing software such as Photoshop or its free version Gimp, or do not have the means to pay 200 or 300 dollars for a professional designer to have a cover.

So, for many people remains the solution to create their cover by themselves, which often results in a visual disaster that can ruin your ebook sales, even if your content is excellent.

But there is another very simple way, that does not require technical skills, nor spending a single dollar. And you'll have a professional looking cover in just ten minutes.

That way is to use the online cover creation service Canva (https://www.canva.com/create/book-covers/).

Simply just insert a background, your text using some text templates the application offers in its free version, and eventually your own images you can upload from your computer.

Once you're done, you will only have to upload your cover that will be created either in high quality PDF format, or in png format with a resolution of 1410 x 2250 pixels, which is very correct and corresponds to the ideal ratio of 1.6 a cover should have.

Here are three examples of covers (in French) I've done in about five minutes each, to show you that you can really have a very good result in no time (they appear in black and white in this version):

Example of cover N°1:

Example of cover N°2:

Example of cover N°3:

If you have a minimum of experience, you can of course make your cover using a software like Gimp (http://www.gimp.org/), which is the free equivalent of Photoshop.

You can get a very good result simply by creating a gradient background, adding an image and playing with the different fonts for your book title.

Contrary to what you may think, there is no need to have an mind blowing design to get a great and successful cover. Some bestsellers covers do not even have pictures, and just play on fonts variations.

If you intend to sell your ebook on the Amazon Kindle platform, Amazon even offers a tool to create your cover live during the upload process of your ebook.

Convert Your Ebook Into The Right Format.

The last step is to convert your ebook in the right format.

There are three main formats for a digital book: the PDF format (.pdf extension), which is the most common, the ePub format (.epub extension) and the Mobi format (.prc or .mobi extension).

To convert your ebook into a PDF format is simple. Most text editors allow it, such as Microsoft Word.

Just save your document as a PDF.

You can also use online converters such as Online2pdf (https://online2pdf.com/).

To convert your ebook into an ePub format, you can use the online converter Online Convert (http://ebook.online-convert.com/convert-to-epub).

To convert your ebook into a Mobi file (the extension will be prc), you can use the free and very convenient Mobipocket Creator software (http://www.mobipocket.com/en/downloadsoft/productd etailscreator.asp)

If you plan to publish your ebook on Amazon Kindle, you can directly convert your ebook into the correct format during the upload process.

You will then have the opportunity to see the result with an online reader, and make changes on your original file in case there would be a display issue.

Once you have converted your ebook into the right format, well, there it is: your ebook is completely finished, completed and ready for sale.

It only remains to congratulate you for your excellent work. If this is your first ebook, you have officially become an author. Congratulations!

CONCLUSION.

Today you have applied a method that allowed you step by step to write an ebook in one weekend, that people will love and especially that is ready to sell.

Unlike other ebook creation approaches, this one will have allowed you to make your book irresistible by managing to maximize its perceived value by the customers, and especially by creating original content without simply copying and pasting articles from others to make a low quality patchwork.

The big advantage is that now that you know this method, you can apply it as soon as you have a free weekend to create other ebooks that your customers will adore and that they will be happy to have bought.

If you do this regularly and create two ebooks per month by blocking two weekends, you will have 24 ebooks at the end of the year.

Just imagine the passive income this can make each month, and you will get an idea of how huge your financial independence can be thanks to what you have learned here.

Although it is not the subject of this book, I offer you a bonus section giving you a number of resources and tools that will allow you to sell effectively, simply and immediately the ebooks you create.

BONUS: WHERE AND HOW TO SELL YOUR EBOOKS.

Create Your Sales Page.

A very good way if you don't want to depend on an external distribution service for your ebook is to create yourself a website with a simple sales page on which your are going to promote your ebook (and the promotion will be very easy if you use the method you've just learnt to create your ebook).

For that, you only need to install Wordpress and create a simple page with a large choice of different templates (free or paid). If you want something very professional, I can recommend you to use for example Optimize Press (you can find it in the form of a theme or plugin for Wordpress), which allows you to create very easily in seconds professional looking sales pages.

You can also directly use services such as Shopify to sell it online without the hassle of creating a website.

Use Online Self-Publishing Platforms.

The other way is to use online self-publishing platforms.

The best one is also the one that holds 80% of the market, which is Amazon.

In a few minutes, your ebook can be published on Amazon Kindle. Simply create an account here: http://kdp.amazon.com/, and upload your book by entering the required information such as your author name or the book description.

You can also use the following platforms:

- Lulu (http://www.lulu.com/publish/ebooks/?cid=us_pubpage_ebooks/)

- Kobo (https://kobo.com/writinglife)

- Nookpress by Barnes & Noble (https://www.nookpress.com/ebooks)

It is needless to spread yourself too thinly. With the tools and addresses you have in this bonus section, you have what is best for making a killing in selling your ebooks.

ABOUT THE AUTHOR.

Remy Roulier is a former computer engineer and marketing manager in a multinational company.

He is now a best-selling author, digital nomad and he travels all around the world, having acquired for over ten years a real expertise in Internet marketing and personal development.

He now shares his tools and experience to allow others to also achieve financial independence and shape their life the way they really want.

CREATIONS FROM THE SAME AUTHOR.

BECOMING RICH IN 42 DAYS:
THE STEP BY STEP METHOD TO MAKE MONEY ONLINE AND LIVE YOUR
DREAMS STARTING FROM SCRATCH.

A proven method that guides you step by step and allows you to achieve your financial independence in 42 days thanks to the Internet, even if you are starting from scratch. A must-read you can't afford missing.

HOW TO CONCENTRATE LIKE EINSTEIN:
THE LAZY STUDENT'S WAY TO INSTANTLY IMPROVE MEMORY & GRADES
WITH THE DOCTOR VITTOZ SECRET CONCENTRATION TECHNIQUE

Concentrate now on what you want as long as you want by learning the never before revealed concentration technique used by Einstein.

RESCUE ACUPRESSURE:
INSTANTLY SUPPRESS STRESS, HEADACHES, MEMORY LAPSES IN
DESPERATE SITUATIONS LIKE DURING AN EXAM

Relieve pain and discomfort immediately when you need it and do not let them make you fail an exam, a job interview or any important moment of your life. 100% practical, very clear and simple, this book is definitely the best investment you can do for your health and success.